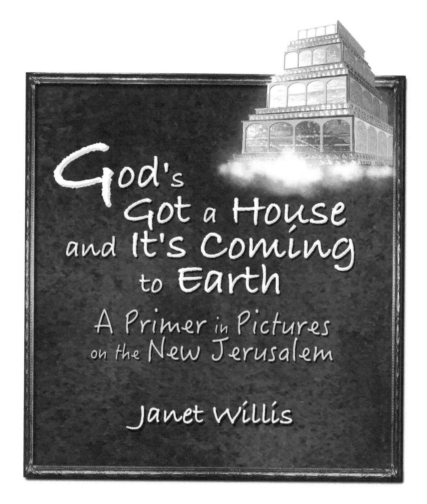

God's Got a House and It's Coming to Earth

A Primer in Pictures on the New Jerusalem

Janet Willis

Illustration Credits

New Jerusalem...Ben Willis, age 10
New Jerusalem pictures on bulletin board:

Micah Willis, age 14, top right
Obediah Willis, age 6, bottom left
Amelia Moody, age 11, bottom right
Eliza Moody, age 6, top left

Crucifixion...Ben Willis, age 11
Resurrection...Joe Willis, age 9
Moses before the Burning Bush...Domenico Fetti, 1613-14
Lamb...Ben Willis, age 5

(all other illustrations by author)

God's Got a House and It's Coming to Earth
A Primer in Pictures on the New Jerusalem
© 2017 Janet Willis
All Rights Reserved

Unless otherwise indicated, Scripture quotations are taken from the New American Standard Bible®, © 1960, 1962, 1963, 1968, 1971, 1972, 1973, 1975, 1977, 1995 by The Lockman Foundation, Used by permission, (www.Lockman.org)/Scripture quotations marked HCSB are taken from the Holman Christian Standard Bible®, Copyright © 1999, 2000, 2002, 2003, 2009 by Holman Bible Publishers. Used by permission. Holman Christian Standard Bible®, Holman CSB®, and HCSB® are federally registered trademarks of Holman Bible Publishers./"Scripture quotations are from the ESV® Bible (The Holy Bible, English Standard Version®), copyright © 2001 by Crossway, a publishing ministry of Good News Publishers. Used by permission. All rights reserved."/Scripture quotations marked KJV are taken from the Holy Bible, King James Version.

www. scottandjanetwillis.com

ISBN-978-0-692-98412-3
LCCN:2017916535
Library of Congress Cataloging-In-Publication Data
Willis, Janet
1. Bible—Prophecy—New Jerusalem   2. Religion—Christian Theology—Eschatology

Khesed Publications
Sebring, Florida

**to my children, grandchildren,
and great grandchildren**

Thank you for your questions

Deuteronomy 6:20

I'm so thankful that
God made a way for us to
all be together in His House
someday! Grandpa is waiting
for us! ☺ Love,
Grandma

We can check out their lives,

When someone speaks for God:

1. Their words agree with what God already said.
   (Deuteronomy 13:1-3)

2. They do miracles in front of witnesses.
   (Deuteronomy 19:15)

3. What they predict is specific and always comes true.
   (Deuteronomy 18:20-22)

4. They are good and faithful servants of God.
   (Matthew 7:15, 16)

They passed every test!

They said
it's a house,
they called it a city.

They said
it's a mountain, but...

"Great is the LORD, and greatly to be praised, in the city of our God, His holy mountain" Psalm 48:1

"the twelve gates were twelve pearls, each one of the gates was a single pearl." Revelation 21:21

THIS one
is pretty!

They spoke of its beauty,
a sight to behold,
We learn of its pearls...

"names were written on them (the gates), which are the names of the twelve tribes of...Israel." Revelation 21:12

of its jewels,
and its gold.

John got a tour,

God took Ezekiel "into the land of Israel...on a very high mountain...on it to the south was a structure like a city...

Ezekiel got a peek,

Behold, there was a man...with a...measuring rod in his hand" Ezekiel 40:2, 3

Don't miss the measurements given by Zeke.

11 miles in length and width

The city "was round about 18,000 measures (or rods) (about 11 miles on each side)" Ezekiel 48:35 KJV

Its length, width, and height from John the Apostle, matches Zeke's size.

It's truly colossal!

11 miles in length, width, and height

The angel "measured the city with the rod" (about 1342 miles) "its length, width, and height are equal" Revelation 21:16

"Things which eye has not seen...and which have not entered the heart of man..." I Corinthians 2:9

But what will it look like? We guess and draw pictures.

Just never forget,
we should only trust Scriptures.

"It had a great and high wall, with twelve gates, and at the gates twelve angels" Revelation 21:12

Who will live there?
Who goes through the gate?

"Blessed are those who wash their robes, so that they may...enter by the gates into the city" Revelation 21:14

"its gates will never be closed...and no one who practices abomination and lying, shall ever come into it..."

There's only one way, we need a clean slate.

"but only those whose names are written in the Lamb's book of life" Revelation 21:25-27 "without shedding of blood there is no forgiveness" Hebrews 9:22

The Lamb shed His blood, the perfect sacrifice, His righteous works get us in Paradise.

"He was afflicted...like a lamb that is led to slaughter" Isaiah 53:7

An angel..."rolled away the stone...sat upon it" and said, "He is not here for He is risen, just as He said." Matthew 28:2,6

Jesus said "because I live, you will live also." John 14:19

He went up to Heaven
to prepare us
a place,
He'll return
with
His house.

What a picture
of grace!

"The day of the LORD is indeed great and very awesome, and who can endure it? Joel 2:11

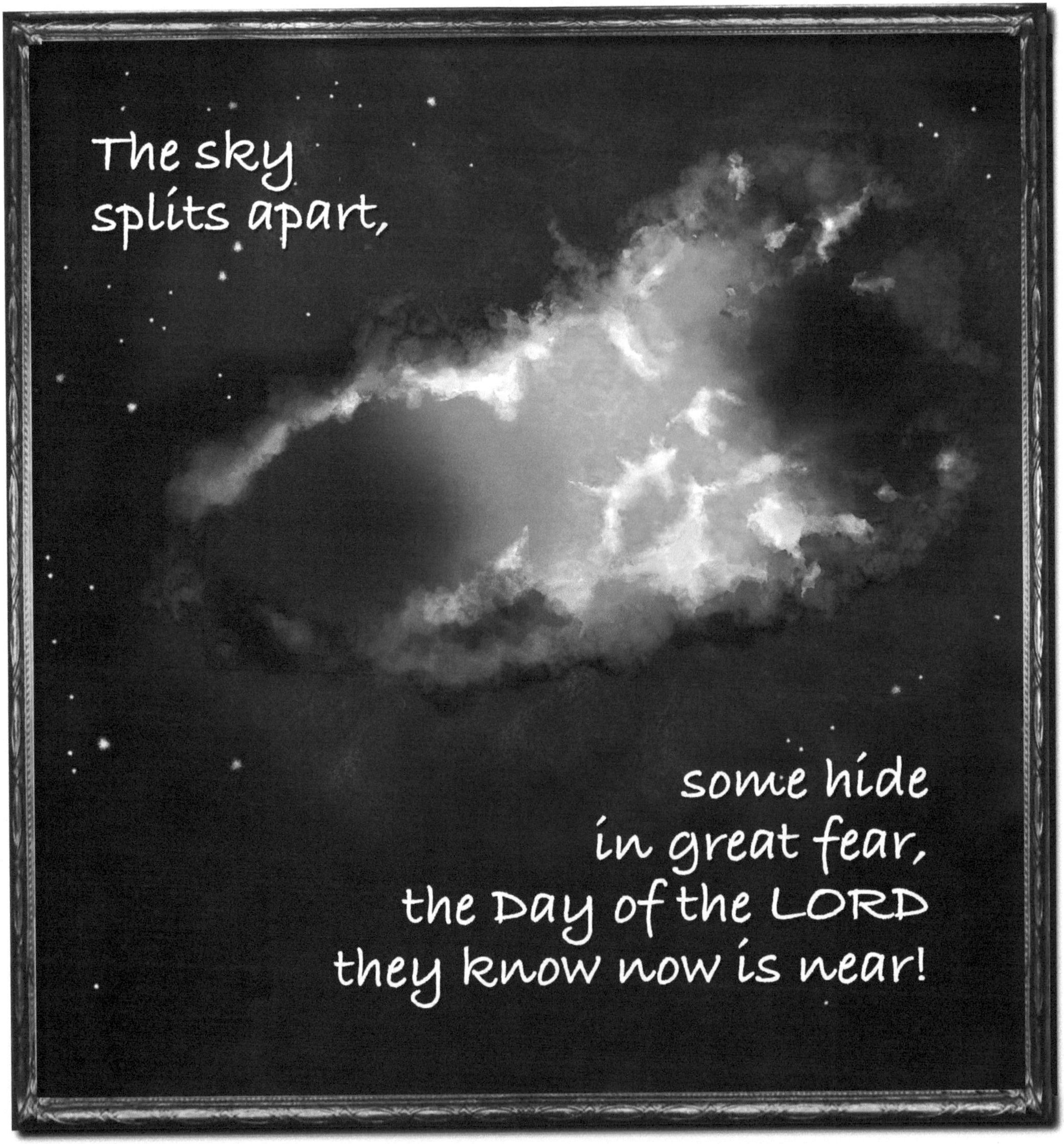

The sky
splits apart,
some hide
in great fear,
the Day of the LORD
they know now is near!

"Men will go into caves of the rocks, And into holes of the ground before the terror of the LORD" Isaiah 2:19

But believers have joy the
whole earth around!
They've been taken up to God
at the trumpet's sound!

"the LORD is about to come out from His place to punish the inhabitants of the earth for their iniquity." Isaiah 26:21

Inside His house, the saved are secure,

"Come, my people, enter into your rooms...hide for a little while until indignation runs its course." Isaiah 26:20

Escaped from
God's wrath,
His promise
is sure!

"Mountains quake because of Him and the hills dissolve; Indeed the earth is upheaved by His presence" Nahum 1:5

A new Temple Mount,
God transforms
the land,

A huge base for His house,
He had it
all planned.

"All the land will be changed into a plain from Geba to Rimmon...but Jerusalem will rise and remain on its site." Zech.14:10

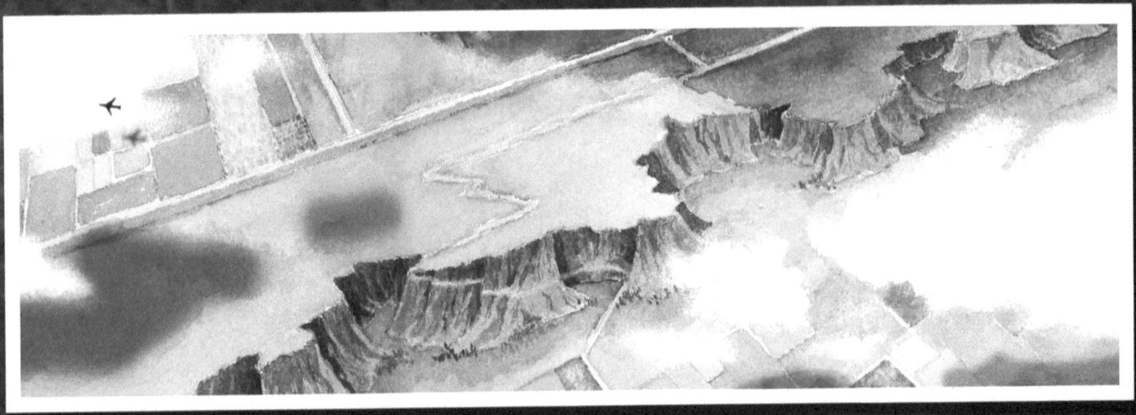

God's city
then lands
right down
on this sod,
It's home
for immortals,
dwelling
with God!

He "will transform our lowly body to be like His glorious body" Philippians 3:21 ESV

New bodies we'll have, every hurt, God will heal,

The dead will be raised imperishable...this mortal will have put on immortality." I Corinthians 15:52-54 "behold, I create new heavens and a new earth...be glad and rejoice forever in what I create." Isaiah 65:17-18

Clean air
and new earth,
all restored, and it's REAL!

"the waters of the (Dead) sea become fresh...fishermen (will have)...a place for the spreading of nets." Ezekiel 47:8-10

"there will be no night there" Revelation 21:25

There's
no night there,
no one's sad
or will weep,

"the city has no need of the sun...for the glory of God has illumined it." Revelation 21:23

The wolf will not harm
all the tender young sheep.

Moses considered "the reproach of Christ greater riches than the treasures of Egypt...

for he was looking to the reward." Hebrews 11:24,26

"On either side of the river was the tree of life, bearing twelve kinds of fruit" Revelation 22:2

And we'll all get to eat from the life-giving Tree.

"I will grant to eat of the tree of life which is in the Paradise of God" Revelation 2:7

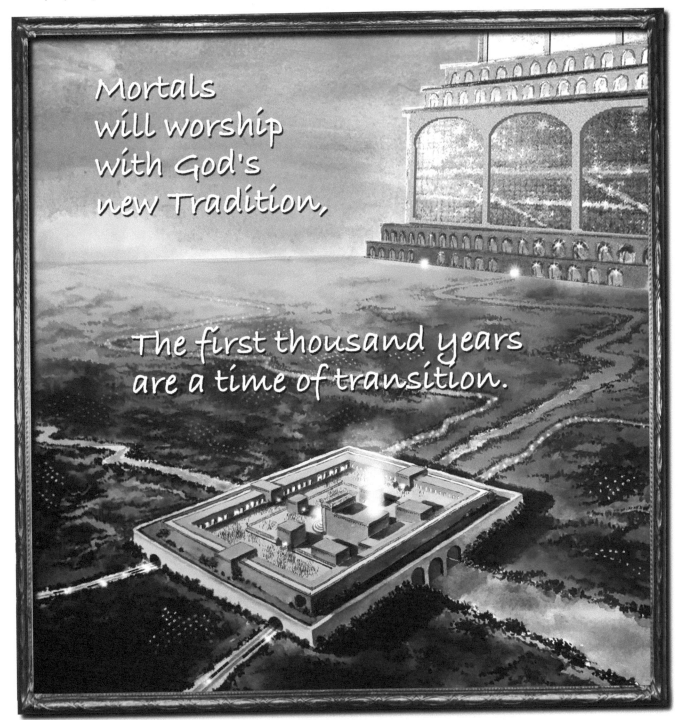

"The people of the land shall also worship...before the LORD on the sabbaths and on the new moons." Ezekiel 46:3

Mortals
will worship
with God's
new Tradition,

The first thousand years
are a time of transition.

"My house will be called a house of prayer for all peoples." Isaiah 56:7

Immortals
will rule
the whole world
throughout,
With jobs that we like,
we'll be out and about.

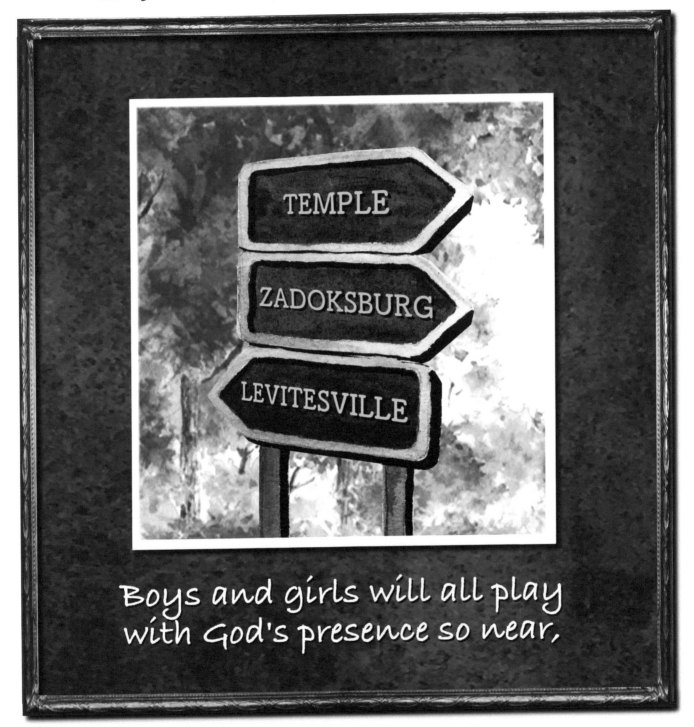

Boys and girls will all play
with God's presence so near,

"And the streets of the city will be filled with boys and girls playing in its streets" Zechariah 8:5

In Jerusalem's streets they'll have nothing to fear.

"they will be secure on their land" Ezekiel 34:27

an angel "holding the key to the abyss and a great chain...laid hold of...the serpent of old, who is the devil...

Those first thousand years,

The Serpent's in chains,

and bound him for 1000 years; and he threw him into the abyss...and sealed it over him" Revelation 20:1-3

"When the 1000 years are completed, Satan will be released" He gathered the nations "together for the war...

Holy Allotment

Levite Neighborhood

Zadok Neighborhood

Temple

Tries
one last attempt,
but our God
HE does reign!

and surrounded...the beloved city...and fire came down from heaven and devoured them." Revelation 20:7-9

The Devil's defeated,
all batches are done,

That SON
Who was promised,
has triumphed
and won!

In Eden, "God said to the Serpent," "(Eve's descendant) shall bruise you on the head" Genesis 3:14,15

The Kingdom's established, God restores what was lost,

Matthew-
Revelation 1-3

You are here

AD

500   1000   1500   2000

Revelation 20 - 22
Revelation 4 - 19

NEW TESTAMENT TIMES

RENAISSANCE 1300

AGE of DISCOVERY
REFORMATION

AMERICAN REVOLUTION 1776

70th WEEK of DANIEL

MILLENNIUM

GREAT WHITE THRONE JUDGMENT

MIDDLE AGES

USA

CHURCH AGE

KINGDOM

Rome

We'll thank Him forever, and remember the cost!

It's Heaven on earth!
Happy ever after!
With joy
in God's
presence,
comfort,
and
laughter!

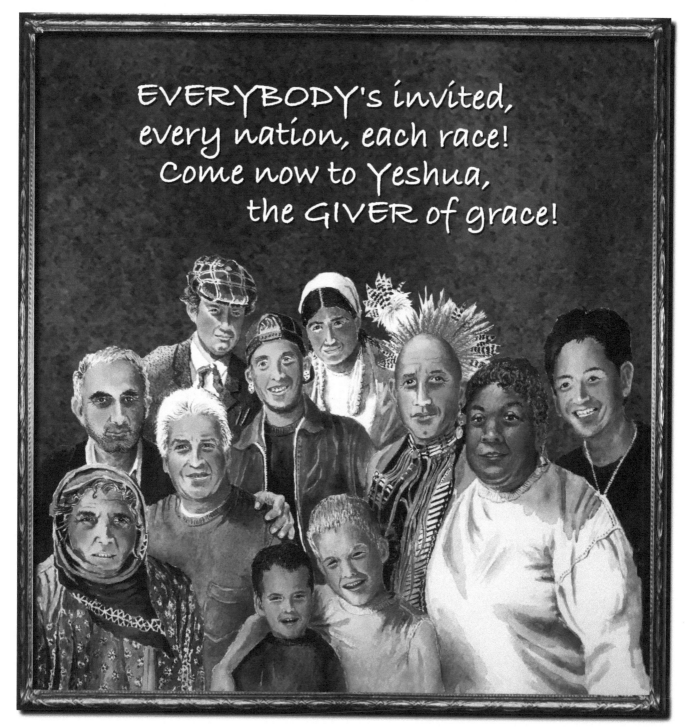

EVERYBODY's invited,
every nation, each race!
Come now to Yeshua,
the GIVER of grace!

God's got a house,
I can't wait to see!

When He comes back to earth,
where will you be?

Dear Reader,

Adversity came into my life in 1994 when I lost six children in a van accident. I knew they were with the Lord where they would be happy and safe and good forever. And I knew I would be with them again someday. But my own loss and indescribable grief drove me toward God, and by His grace, I drank in His Word, the Bible. In the weeks that followed, things about heaven jumped off the page. I saw how the heroes of the faith found strength to endure trials. "They were looking for a city whose builder and maker is God" (Hebrews 11:10). That heavenly city, new Jerusalem is now above but will someday come down to this earth. I began to pay attention to prophecies about Jerusalem that are yet to be fulfilled. "For the LORD has chosen Zion...this is My resting place forever; Here I will dwell, for I have desired it"(Psalm 132:13-14).

I wrote this verse in a notebook, along with many others. Questions arose about the size, the shape, and the timing of when this city would arrive. I wanted to be accurate to what God actually said. I needed to dig deep. It became a treasure hunt, a quest. As I checked cross references and compared Scripture with Scripture I began to comprehend more than ever the incredible goodness of God. I realized He had graciously revealed far more information about our eternal destination than I ever thought.

I saw how God gave Ezekiel a look into the future. He was transported to a high plateau in Israel. On it to the south, he saw "a structure like a city"(Ezekiel 40:2). He saw a temple in the middle of this Holy Allotment, and it was separate from the city. The city had three gates on each side, and the gates were named for the twelve tribes of Israel. Ezekiel's angelic tour guide gave the size of the city on each side: approximately 11 miles. Not only that, but he said, "The name of the city from that day shall be the LORD is there" (Ezekiel 48:35).

John also got a look into the future (Revelation 21-22). He saw a city descending to this earth and it had three gates on each side, named for the twelve tribes of Israel. It sounded like the city Ezekiel described. Then I noticed right after giving the number 12,000 stadia (approximately 1342 miles), God says the length, the width, and the height are equal (Revelation 21:16).

I always assumed John meant 1342 miles in each direction, but what if he meant that number was the total? When I multiplied 11 miles in length x 11 miles in width x 11 miles in height, it came to 1331 cubic miles. I was stunned! John's measurements matched up with Ezekiel's! Puzzle pieces from all over the Bible began to fall in place. Size was the key!

Jesus said His Father's house has many dwelling places (John 14:2). That also sounds like what Ezekiel described: a single structure that is a city! Throughout the Bible, I saw how God's dwelling place is often called God's Holy Mountain. I thought, "Maybe God meant what He said." Maybe the "structure like a city", the Father's house that has "many dwelling places" is shaped like a mountain. Then I saw the New Testament directly compares the New Jerusalem to Mount Sinai (Hebrews 12:18-27). I began to grasp what on earth Heaven might be like. Truly, His Word is a treasure to be mined!

Since I am an artist, my fingers itched to try to depict the many word pictures God had given. I knew I would never have certainty until I see it with my own eyes, but I was looking for Biblically-based possibilities. Eventually a full account of my research was published in the book What on Earth Is Heaven Like? This read-aloud picture book can be used as an introduction to that book.

The New Jerusalem is the destination for anyone who repents of their sin and puts their faith in God's Messiah, Jesus (Romans 10:13). And someday, it will be the capital city of King Jesus on this earth. All God's promises will be fulfilled. What a powerful, proactive, permanent love God has for us, for those who trust in Him!

Grateful to Jesus,
Janet Willis